Silver Burdett Picture Histories

The Days of the Musketeers

Pierre Miquel
Illustrated by Claude and Denise Millet

Translated by LinguAssist
from La Vie privée des Hommes: Au temps des Mousquetaires
first published in France in 1978 by
Librairie Hachette, Paris

© Librairie Hachette, 1978. Adapted and published in the
United States by Silver Burdett Company, Morristown, N.J. 1985 Printing.

ISBN 0-382-06923-4
Library of Congress Catalog Card No. 81-52602

Contents

In the days of the musketeers

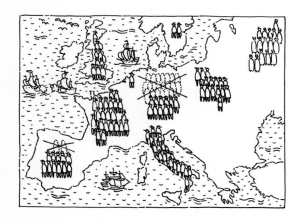

Population of the principal European countries in the 17th century
France *Approximately 17,000,000 inhabitants*
Russia *11,000,000 inhabitants*
Austria *7,500,000 inhabitants*
Brandenburg-Prussia *2,000,000 inhabitants*
England *7,500,000 inhabitants (including Wales and Scotland)*
Spain *8,500,000 inhabitants at the beginning of the century 6,500,000 at the end*
Italy *13,000,000 inhabitants*
Poland *16,000,000 inhabitants*
Scandinavia *(Sweden, Norway, Denmark, and Finland) 2,000,000 inhabitants*
Dutch Republic *(United Provinces) 2,000,000 inhabitants*

THE EUROPEAN POWERS

In the 17th century the most populated country in Europe was France. France had a population of approximately 17 million people. Spain, however, was the richest nation in Europe. Although the population of Spain itself was only about 8 million, at one time the king of Spain ruled over nearly 13 million other Europeans—Flemings, Italians, and natives of Franche-Comté—as well as millions of subjects in Spanish colonies in the Americas. Every year convoys of ships delivered 300 tons of pure silver from America to the Spanish king in Seville. Riches from the New World enabled him to maintain the largest armies and buy the most deadly weapons in Europe.

In addition to the Catholic powers of Spain, France, Savoy, Venice, and Austria, the powerful Protestant states of England, Holland, Sweden, and certain German principalities now emerged. And in far-off orthodox Russia, the czars were attempting to increase their territorial holdings in order to compete with the Swedes.

Maritime rivalries also abounded. In the Baltic the Dutch owned most of the merchant ships that normally called upon the Hanseatic ports, which were free German cities. In their large ships the Dutch transported most of the heavy cargo, including salt, minerals, and wood, in the Baltic and North seas as well as in the Atlantic. The Spanish, Swedish, Norwegians, and Bretons conceded that the Dutch were undoubtedly the most powerful nation on the seas.

Nevertheless, the English navy challenged the Dutch domination of the seas. In fifty years the English navy had doubled its tonnage. England had devoted half its budget to the construction of a formidable naval force, whose mission was to protect the rapidly expanding English merchant fleet. Fierce battles took place in the western seas. The English navy waged war against Holland, France, and Spain. Spanish galleons, loaded with cargoes of silver and gold, were attacked by English pirates more often now than they had been in the 16th century.

Vessels built in France on the orders of Richelieu under Louis XIII and Colbert under Louis XIV played an important part in this fearful warfare of the seas. Pirates from Dunkirk and Saint-Malo in France were just as skillful at raiding galleons as the English.

A GOLDEN FLOOD

Gold from the New World always fascinated the Old World. The desire of the rich and aristocratic for luxury items stimulated industry and contributed to the flow of the precious yellow metal into Europe. The development of royal and manorial courts encouraged the growth of many luxury-related industries. The textile industry thrived in both Holland and Spanish Flanders. Woolens and velvets from Amsterdam were shipped to many places throughout Europe. Every year England exported three-quarters of the wool it produced. Amsterdam and London were the most important financial centers in all of Europe.

Wars and the vaulting ambitions of princes were other factors that served to increase Europe's need for gold from the Spanish colonies. Great numbers of Spaniards left their farms to join Spain's armies. Thousands of Germans, Swiss, and Scots were also soldiers in the Spanish armies. These soldiers had to be paid and fed. Spain's deserted farms could no longer supply the food its people and its armies required. Less and less wheat, rye, and other crops were being grown and harvested. Soon the shortage of food became so severe that the Spanish kings had to import food from other countries. And so the flow of gold from Spain to the rest of Europe began to increase.

Large quantities of wood, iron, and copper were needed to build cannons and ships. The Germans and French prospected for iron and copper. The English discovered uses for coal. All of Europe mined its mountains and built arsenals. The great forests were felled and the wood used to build warships. Industry and trade grew, gold flowed, and Europe became rich.

Europe's fleets

- *In Holland 10,000 sailors on 500 ships fished for herring.*
- *The size of the English merchant fleet increased from 7,000 tons in 1580 to 115,000 tons in 1629. It reached 340,000 tons in 1686.*
- *In 1683 the French navy had 5,619 cannons, as compared to 8,400 belonging to the English fleet.*
- *France possessed 18 oceangoing vessels in 1660 and 120 in 1670!*

RURAL AND INDUSTRIAL EUROPE

Despite its industrial progress, most areas of Europe remained basically rural. Although 500,000 people were now living in London, 5 million Englishmen were still farmers.

In France most of the population of 17 million were farmers. Grain and wines from France were sold abroad, mostly to Spain. Numerous ships from Brittany carried wines from Bordeaux or the Loire to ports in the North Sea. The Dutch were great

consumers of French wines. On return trips the ships carried cargoes of nails, candles, lead, iron, soap, linens, and woolens back to Brittany.

France had to import such large quantities of industrial products that from the beginning of the 17th century, the French realized the need for establishing factories and mills in their own territories. In exchange for Dutch woolens, English linen, Swedish iron and wood, Venetian glass, and Flemish tapestries, too much gold and silver was leaving the kingdom. Sully under Henry IV, Richelieu under Louis XIII, and Colbert under Louis XIV all encouraged the development of industry in France. They wanted the army and navy to be equipped with weapons, ammunition, uniforms, and other materials all made in France. A great many foundries to manufacture cannons and cannonballs were built, and arsenals were created in the military harbors of Toulon, Dunkirk, Rochefort, and Brest. At the same time, luxury products, such as the magnificent tapestries of the Gobelin works in Paris, were also being made.

Just like the English and the Dutch, the French began to engage in colonial trade, establishing trading companies and building forts overseas. The exploitation of the West Indies began, and plantations in the Antilles sent their sugar back to France, the mother country. Because of this rush for the wealth of the New World, trade in the Mediterranean decreased.

POORLY DISTRIBUTED WEALTH

The populations of most European countries remained largely unconscious of the great changes going on around them. Only the middle classes of northwestern Europe and the great Spanish nobles grew richer. The common people, who made up the majority of the population, were concerned only with the problems of survival. A year with too much or too little rain, or a storm at the wrong time of summer could threaten a whole area with famine. Only the middle classes and the wealthier farmers had the reserves to tide them over. When wheat or rye was scarce, the peasants had to make do with bread made from barley or oats. When grain was no longer available, villagers dug up ferns and made bread with the roots. If necessary, they even ate crushed acorns! Often, the children died young. Half the babies born did not live to reach their first birthday. The average life expectancy was about twenty-two years. Two centuries were to pass before the descendants of these peasants were able to live without the constant threat of dying from hunger.

In addition to the suffering from hunger and from cold during hard winters, large-scale epidemics wrought havoc on the population. In the cities, one out of every two people fell victim to the plague. Diseases such as dysentery—a bacterial disease spread by polluted water—killed hundreds of thousands of people. Other diseases from which people commonly suffered included gout, smallpox, and various poorly identified fevers. The rapid spread of deadly diseases was due largely to the lack of a balanced diet and very poor hygiene. Only leprosy, a curse of the Middle Ages, regressed.

ROBBING AND LOOTING SOLDIERS

The 17th century was a time of almost continuous warfare. Troops on maneuvers pilfered and killed. Soldiers were feared by peasants throughout Europe. In France the musketeers of the king frolicked along the roads, wearing silver swords and bands of lace, and terrorizing the peasants. Many soldiers turned to banditry following their discharge from the army. It did not matter to the peasants whether their persecutors were still soldiers or had turned to marauding after leaving the army—the common people were still victims.

RELIGIOUS WARS

Civil wars were even more dreadful than foreign ones. Protestants and Catholics continued to fight with one another in England, and especially in France. The Edict of Nantes, issued in 1598 under Henry IV of France, granted freedom of worship to the Protestants. In spite of this, Louis XIII later disturbed the uneasy peace by demanding that the Protestants surrender their fortified cities. The king sent military expeditions to conquer the Protestant armies and force the peasants to convert to Catholicism. With the help of England and certain German princes, the Protestants were able to mount a long resistance.

Seemingly endless religious conflict raged throughout Europe. When the king of Spain crossed

---

The price of a painting

Rubens (1577–1640) was one of the greatest Dutch painters.
Here are the prices he asked for some of the paintings produced in his studio:
Prometheus Bound .... 500 florins
Christ on the Cross .... 500 florins
The Last Judgment ....1,200 florins
Saint Sebastian .... 300 florins
Daniel in the Lion's
Den .... 600 florins
During the same period, a craftsman in Holland earned 15 florins a month.

the Franche-Comté region or subdued a rebellion in Spanish Flanders, he also persecuted the Protestants. In order to escape capture and punishment, Protestants sometimes disguised themselves as beggars and sought refuge in the forests.

POLITICAL UNREST

The ideas and practices of absolute rule by a supreme sovereign eventually aroused strong opposition in western Europe. The Dutch Netherlands, led by the province of Holland, was the first to rebel. In 1648 the Dutch Netherlands gained independence and became a land of refuge for many of those liberals who were persecuted throughout Europe. Philosophers and politicians were among those who found a safe haven there.

In England, rebellion roared against the absolutism of the king, Charles I. Catholics, Anglicans, Scottish Presbyterians, and the uncompromising Puritans fought bitter battles throughout England. The Puritans followed Oliver Cromwell, who established a parliamentary republic and had Charles I publicly executed for treason in London on January 30, 1649.

France was not spared by the wave of political unrest sweeping Europe. As far back as the reign of Louis XIII, the rich middle classes of the large cities and the nobles whose privileges were threatened by the monarchy incited popular uprisings in Paris in an attempt to recover their powers. The "Fronde," as this uprising of all classes was called, made it necessary for the king to reconquer his own capital. Cardinal Richelieu went to war against the rebellious lords, destroying their castles and beheading them if they dared to resist his policies. Later, with flexibility and determination, Cardinal Mazarin, first minister to the young king Louis XIV, overcame the resistance of the members of parliament and the upper-middle classes. Mazarin, as Richelieu before him, led the fight for a strong monarchy, which would no longer be at the mercy of different factions.

In all countries the common people were the ones who paid the highest price for this cruel confrontation between the dominant classes of society. Ordinary people everywhere were burdened by the taxes of the state as well as any levied by the local lords or churches. They existed totally without financial security.

Some large cities

London
500,000 inhabitants
Seville
100,000 inhabitants
Amsterdam
180,000 inhabitants
Naples
280,000 inhabitants
Paris
400,000 inhabitants
Madrid
100,000 inhabitants
Venice
148,000 inhabitants
Marseille
50,000 inhabitants

Six million city dwellers

No sewers, no sidewalks, and almost no paved roads!
The streets of the large European cities were dingy, overcrowded, and dangerous places. They were congested with animals and strewn with garbage. In the 17th century, only 6 million people lived in Europe's cities. Only 12 cities had populations of more than 100,000. Most cities were small—only 10 to 20 thousand people. They were often still surrounded by walls and dominated by the manor of a nobleman. The growth of the urban population, notably in London, Paris, and Amsterdam was, however, a sure indication that greater numbers of people were beginning to leave the countryside.

Nevertheless, the cities remained basically unchanged from medieval times. Wooden houses in London burned like matchsticks during the great fire of 1666. In 1597 an earthquake engulfed three streets in Lisbon. The lightweight buildings could not withstand the tremors and crumbled to the ground. In the mean cob houses that lined the narrow streets, people lived crowded together without sanitary facilities. In Lyon, France, for example, a workingman's family of seven or eight lived crowded into only 30 square meters of space!

Paris was usually short of water. The city's pumps and cisterns could barely provide one liter of water per day for each inhabitant. There were no streetlamps in Paris. In order to light the streets, the city distributed more than 6,000 candle lanterns to the people to place in their windows. There were no paid street cleaners and people had to clean their own walkways.

However, some European cities were beginning to enjoy the benefits of organized urban planning. In Madrid tall houses with large windows were built along wide avenues. In Amsterdam the number of buildings tripled over 40 years. In Paris, also, beautiful stone buildings were constructed near the Pont Neuf. And the handsome Place Royale became a center of attraction. Yet there were some cities, such as Naples, which continued their undisciplined growth.

A merchant sells blown glass on a city street in Italy.

Large cities were plagued by beggars and robbers. Pickpockets stole purses and jewelry from people on the streets. The still poorly organized police rarely had a chance to catch the criminals before they sold their loot in the thieves' quarter of the city.

This knife grinder has set up shop in the Saint-Germain market in Paris. Behind him is the stall of a coffee merchant. For two cents a cup he sold a beverage that was originally considered a tonic. Soon, however, coffee became a part of everyday life.

In the cities the various small trades included billposters, water carriers, delivery people, fruit and vegetable merchants, and knife grinders. Carts were too wide to travel up and down many of the narrow streets, so home deliveries were made on men's backs.

In Paris the Pont-Neuf, a bridge completed during the reign of Henry IV, made it easier for the inhabitants of the left bank to reach the gates of the Louvre. Wealthy people traveled in carriages or sedan chairs, with coachmen clearing a path through the crowds with their whips. There were always crowds on the bridge, because it was a very popular place to meet, and the city's idlers were attracted there by the stalls, jugglers, and magicians. The sidewalks were four steps high to protect pedestrians from traffic.

Theater and entertainment

The working-class population of Flanders enjoyed fun and festivity, as shown in the picture below. Fairs provided occasions for them to celebrate. Barrels of beer and wine were opened and merchants sold waffles, sugar almonds, and gingerbread. Festivals were held on bridges or at fairgrounds. The crowds loved the entertainment provided by strolling players, jugglers, magicians, trained animal acts, and puppet shows.

People also enjoyed going to public parks. In Paris the Cours-la-Reine with its four elm-lined walks was a meeting place for the very fashionable, who paraded through in emblazoned coaches. Some went there at midnight surrounded by musicians and footmen carrying torches. People strolled through the beautiful Tuileries gardens or the bois de Boulogne, a wood northwest of Paris. In this wild place one could still hunt deer, and from time to time the king would come here to attend military inspections. On Sundays many Parisians relaxed in the outdoor cafes on the Bièvre River, visited the Gobelin tapestry works, or frequented the taverns of villages outside the city. A stroll through the vineyards of Rueil or Meudon was also a pleasant way to spend a Sunday.

One of the most popular forms of entertainment was the theater. Large audiences attended performances in the theaters of London. Parisians acclaimed the plays and performances of Molière, a famous dramatist and comic actor.

The popularity of the theater also spread to central and eastern parts of Europe. In Moscow a theater might be set up in a nobleman's house and plays performed there. The Russians also enjoyed watching puppet shows and happily applauded the players.

Traveling theater companies performed in many of the provincial cities as well as in the capitals. Some even set up their stages and performed in small villages

Performers entertaining an audience in the Netherlands

The crowds enjoyed all kinds of shows. Above, townspeople gather to watch a cruel game in which a goose is suspended from an overhead rope. The desperate bird honks and flaps its wings and the people cheer as a blindfolded man tries to cut off the bird's head.

On certain days there was a festival at the expense of the pope. According to a custom dating back to the Renaissance, wine poured from the fountains, and a whole steer was roasted on a spit to the delight of the Italian townspeople.

From the 15th century on, itinerant actors traveled the roads of Europe with their costumes and stage properties. They set up their stages on village greens and tennis courts, in marketplaces, innyards, and the courtyards or halls of noblemen's palaces—anywhere they could gain entry. They rehearsed wherever they could and performed whenever the reward might be sufficient.

Louis XIV of France celebrated his conquest of Franche-Comté with festivities that lasted from July 4 to August 31, 1674. On August 18, the day began with a meal served in the park at Versailles. Later the court watched a performance of *Iphigénie,* a play by Racine. The day ended with a brilliant fireworks display.

English gentlemen exiled by Cromwell discovered croquet and other outdoor sports while in France. French gentlemen, though, often preferred an indoor game similar to modern-day tennis called jeu de paume. Many cities and even private mansions had a hall especially set up for this popular game.

Masters, journeymen, and apprentices

No unemployed in the trade guilds! In order to limit competition and insure consistent quality in their work, craftsmen restricted access to their professions by training very few workers in their trade. Not just anyone could open up shop and be a jeweler, a butcher, or a tailor. You first had to be declared a "master" in your guild. In any trade, you began first as an apprentice. Apprentices signed a contract with their master in front of a notary. The master provided his apprentices with bed, board, and clothing, as well as teaching them his trade. In return apprentices were required to work for the master for a certain length of time. Once an apprentice learned a trade he was a "journeyman." It often took a long time to become a journeyman—one year for a clog-maker, two for a carpenter, four for a printer, and five for a surgeon. The title of master was not easy to obtain since special rules were established that only allowed sons to follow their fathers. Therefore apprentices outside of the family had very little hope of becoming more than journeymen.

In some trades a family would pay a master to take their child on as an apprentice. In Paris a trimming manufacturer demanded 30 pounds. This was a difficult trade that involved hand embroidering materials, braids, and tassels with gold and silver thread. These embellishments were used to decorate furnishings, like canopies and curtains. In Versailles the queen had the ornaments in her room changed every five years. When the winter ornaments of crimson velvet embroidered with gold from Louis XIV's room were discarded and burned, a total of 3 ingots of precious metal weighing 60 kilos were recovered from the fire.

Seventeenth-century craftsmen did not manufacture luxury items only. On the contrary, most of the things they produced were objects used in everyday life—clothes, shoes, wigs, tableware, furniture, and tools. The humbler craftsmen, such as carpenters and shoemakers, were often ill housed and fed and often died in debt.

The workshop of a trimming manufacturer

This rope maker has a clump of hemp around his waist. By hand he turns the hemp into string, and then turns the string into rope. He works with the hemp under the trees to shelter it from wind, sun, and rain. The hemp must be kept dry during the whole operation.

Peasants grew hemp everywhere in Europe. Hemp ropes were widely used in many industries, such as shipping, transportation, and public works. Anjou and Piedmont were great hemp-producing regions.

The wool trade was one of the main sources of England's wealth. Pictured here are two steps in the process of cloth making. The worker in the background uses a teasle to draw up the loose fibers in the cloth. The cloth shearer cuts off these loose fibers.

The organ builders' trade was one of the most delicate of all. These craftsmen had to make minute adjustments to the pipe openings to obtain the desired notes. The great organs came from Germany or England. Excellent organs were also built in France and Italy.

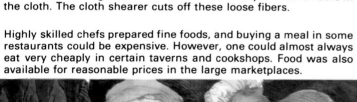

Highly skilled chefs prepared fine foods, and buying a meal in some restaurants could be expensive. However, one could almost always eat very cheaply in certain taverns and cookshops. Food was also available for reasonable prices in the large marketplaces.

Many everyday objects were made of wood. This journeyman woodworker uses a pedal-powered lathe to turn a piece of wood as his child watches from a small movable pen. This craftsman may be working on a commission from a cabinetmaker.

Mines, mills, and shipyards

In Holland, western Germany, England, and France, mechanized industry made great progress during the 17th century. German technicians were well-known in the mining industry. They directed operations throughout central and eastern Europe, from Bohemia to Russia. In Belgium, England, and the Rhine Valley, iron metallurgy was developing rapidly. The English and Belgians already knew how to manufacture cast iron, and by the end of the century, the first blast furnaces using coke were operating in England.

While the techniques of metallurgy were progressing in foundries, there were considerable developments in the glass industry, especially in Italy and Holland. The Venetians manufactured thin glass plates 70 centimeters long that could be cut with a diamond. In the Saint-Gobain forest in France, Abraham Thévart opened a workshop to make glass near deposits of pure silica, a mineral used in its manufacture.

Throughout Europe, the manufacture of textiles was the most developed industry. Flanders, Normandy, and particularly England dominated the wool textile industry. In the French city of Beauvais, there were more than 700 looms in operation, and during the century the production of woolen fabric increased fourfold in the Netherlands.

Warships and merchant ships were being built in Europe's busy shipyards. The most modern shipyards were in Rotterdam. Windmills were used to power the sawmills that produced the wood for the ships. Windmills also powered the tall cranes that were used in the construction of the famous large, narrow-sterned cargo ships capable of navigating in shallow waters. In Amsterdam, the shipyards of one trading company alone employed more than a thousand workers.

In the royal factories, machinery and production methods were sometimes more traditional. Members of the French court visited the Gobelin tapestry works to watch and admire the skillful workers weaving extraordinary tapestries, working against the light and watching the results in a mirror.

16

A tapestry being woven horizontally at the Gobelin factory

The royal tobacco factory of Mexico. Since the 16th century, tobacco had become increasingly popular in Europe. It was first imported from America, but eventually was grown in Europe also. Some governments tried to prohibit its use, but in time took over the industry.

In 1657 the Dutchman Christian Huygens invented the pendulum clock and the spiral spring that allowed for regulating the swinging of the pendulum. The clock industry underwent considerable development throughout Europe, especially in Switzerland.

This worker has poured molten copper into a bucket filled with water. By plunging birch rods into the water, his assistant obtained beads of the metal. In this form, copper mixes better with silver, and the alloy obtained in this way is easy to work with.

Mining required a large work force. At the bottom of the shafts, miners loaded ore into huge buckets that were brought to the surface by winches turned by a donkey or by men. The buckets were emptied into wheelbarrows that the workers transported to the foundry. In the

Since the 15th century, cannons had been cast in one piece of bronze. Each cannon of the same series contained the same amount of metal. By weighing the cannons, workers verified the quality of the product. Artillery was of great importance on the battlefields.

mining industry, even in western Europe, trade guilds did not exist, and men worked in unsafe conditions. Nevertheless, mining became more and more important—iron and copper were needed in the foundries to cast the kings' cannons.

Wealthy merchants and bankers

Dutch and English bankers gradually replaced Italian money changers. The two great financial centers of Europe were Amsterdam and London. The Amsterdam stock exchange was the center for commodities trading. Here, trading prices of the merchandise dealt in were posted. Grain, linens, and mining products thus had an international quotation. A speculator in Amsterdam said he could make 100,000 rixdalers (A rixdaler was an old silver coin, the value of which was about one dollar.) if he learned of the death of the king of Spain a few hours before the news reached the exchange.

As well as dealing with private individuals, the banks also did business with governments and trading companies. These companies were quoted on the stock exchanges in Amsterdam and London. Bonds issued by cities and provinces were also traded on the stock exchanges.

In France and Spain, business was less prosperous. Spanish noblemen, like their king, spent lavishly without counting the cost. They minted money with gold and silver from America and squandered it in Europe. But as the quantities of precious metal they received began to decrease, money became more scarce. Spain had not taken advantage of the fabulous wealth from America to build up business or banking systems. In France the fortunes made in manufacturing and business were not always reinvested in industry. Many times, the wealthy preferred to buy land or titles.

The king of France sold parts of his authority—for £500 one could buy a notary's office. In much the same way, one could become a clerk, harbor officer, or meat or cheese inspector. In order to recover their investment, these newly promoted officials demanded fees and bribes from those who required their services. During Corneille's time, it was not advisable to visit any royal agent without bringing him a present.

The office of a Dutch government agent

After the resumption of religious persecution of French Protestants, many Protestant industrialists, particularly those in the textile industry, chose to go into exile. Some settled in Brandenburg, where they built mills and factories. Their fine products sold very well.

The Dutch bankers developed a very elaborate accounting system. It allowed them to perform the various money conversion operations and assured their firms of high profits. Banks hired more and more well-qualified and experienced personnel.

Privateers stalked large merchant ships on the high seas. When an English privateer returned to the port of London with his plunder, the seized merchandise was unloaded and an inventory was taken. A portion of the loot was paid to the king, who then authorized the release of the goods. The rest of the cargo would be auctioned off. After the state took its share of the profits, the rest was divided up with two thirds going to the ship's owner, and one third to the captain and the crew.

Thanks to gold and silver from the New World, there was an abundance of money in Europe. Many mints were created to turn out English guineas, French louis, and Spanish maravedis. The only way to establish an acceptable rate of exchange was to weigh the coins.

The minting of money in royal workshops was done with a coining press instead of a hammer, making the coins uniform in shape. This reduced the circulation of counterfeit coins. Since these were still stamped with a hammer, they could be easily recognized.

Buildings of brick and stone

In 1666 a terrible fire devastated London. The Parliament buildings, churches, and 1,300 dwellings burned to the ground and had to be rebuilt. It took the city 10 years to rise again from its ashes. In rebuilding, architects used more bricks and less wood to help prevent another catastrophe. Some architects also made plans for organized city development, but the public showed little interest in perspective or in the proposed wide, straight avenues. While large buildings did have to conform to certain regulations, buildings of three floors or less were exempt. And since most people did not really want to change the face of their city, many of the narrow streets of the past were rebuilt.

In many European cities, stone was in short supply. Even brick, which was used extensively on buildings in Amsterdam and in the reconstruction of London, was not readily available everywhere. Nevertheless, construction efforts intensified. In Amsterdam, for example, the urban area tripled in 40 years.

Louis XIV enriched Paris by constructing Les Invalides, a home for disabled soldiers, the colonnade of the Louvre, the Saint-Martin and Saint-Denis gates, and public squares, like the place des Victoires and the place Vendôme. The Saint-Roch hill was leveled and stone quays were built along the waterfront. Even though beautiful mansions were built in areas like the Marais, we must not forget that much of Paris remained a city of wood and cob.

Throughout the European capitals, many churches and cathedrals were constructed. In the 17th century the baroque style of architecture was popular. Richly decorated churches, like Saint-Etienne-du-Mont in Paris, the Gesu in Rome, and Salzburg Cathedral, required the mobilization of large labor forces. Masons and stonecutters built their huts on the construction sites. Carpenters put up huge scaffolds, which were needed for the construction of heavy lead-covered domes and the installation of enormous stone blocks on building facades. The laborers who worked at these jobs had no accident insurance.

The reconstruction of St. Paul's Cathedral in London following the fire of 1666. Christopher Wren was the architect.

Major construction at the Louvre. This picture shows the building of the famous colonnade designed by the architect Claude Perrault. To bring the giant stones for the ornamental facade to the site, machines to transport and hoist the stones had to be built. An army of workers was required for this job. Heavy beams that rolled on oak logs enclosed the stone. When the whistle blew, the men pulled on the levers with ropes and the stone moved slowly. It was raised and set into place with the aid of giant hoists.

In Paris to build squares lined with beautiful houses, architects used such uniform building materials as brick and limestone. The houses of the place Royale arcades all look alike. In the central square, vegetable gardens were planted instead of trees.

In Madrid the kings of Spain used town-planning techniques to develop their city. There were wide tree-lined avenues and large public squares. The Puerto del Sol became the center of town. At the new fountain, women fetched water, which flowed day and night.

The Dutch and Italians were the uncontested masters of glass working. Rather than being fitted with a single pane, house windows were constructed of many small glass panes joined together by lead seams. Often, some of the panes were made from stained glass.

The importance of agriculture

In Europe eight men out of ten worked the land. Bread made up 80 percent of their diet. To grow the wheat needed to make enough bread, practically every bit of available land was planted. Sometimes the yields were very low because crops were planted on land that was barely suitable for farming. There was very little grazing land for cattle. In Normandy, which is presently a rich cattle-raising region, 90 percent of the land was ploughed and planted.

The potato was still a curiosity from America. Corn, also introduced to Europe from America, was grown only in Portugal, and rice was not yet grown in Spain or Italy. However, the Europeans did grow many other grains, such as barley, rye, and buckwheat. In Mediterranean areas where few cattle were raised, the land was overrun by huge herds of sheep and goats, which destroyed the vegetation.

However, rich agricultural regions did begin to develop in Europe. Methods were developed that helped to improve the quality of the soil. This led to the increased cultivation of vegetable crops. With the abundance of crops, marketplaces to sell the vegetables were created in the cities. The Dutch cultivated commercial crops, such as flax, tobacco, and oilseeds. They also grew hops, which were used to manufacture beer. The rich residue of the brewing process was fed to the cattle.

The English cultivated hitherto unused land and enriched the soil with fertilizer. In Suffolk they developed dairy and vegetable farming to feed the people of London. The Danes also worked to create fine dairy cattle.

Some attempts at new methods of agriculture were made in France and Germany. But on the whole, farming in these areas remained bound to the old techniques. Yields were low, and the people dreaded the harsh climate that could cause great famines. From the Atlantic to the Urals, the survival of the people of Europe depended almost entirely on the weather.

A German peasant and his wife smoke their evening pipes.

Canals lined with windmills crisscrossed the Dutch countryside. In the 16th and 17th centuries, windmills pumped water from lakes as large as 17,000 acres. The reclaimed land was immediately fertilized and planted.

In the spring, French villagers joyously raised a May tree. The ribbon-trimmed tree was a symbol of strength and prosperity. At this time, feasts with dancing and music celebrated the real beginning of the agricultural year.

From November to March, Italian peasants gathered water willows on the marshy plains of the Po River. The slender stalks were pruned, soaked, and peeled in preparation for weaving the pliable rods into baskets and other practical objects.

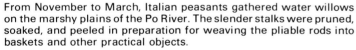

Boats and carts brought thousands of cheeses to the markets in Alkmaar and Gouda in Holland. The big, dense balls of cheese stayed fresh for long periods. Holland's fine dairy cows still produce milk for the famous Dutch cheeses.

Net fishing was less productive in the Mediterranean than in the North Sea. But the people of southern Italy made use of all the resources available to them. They fished for mullet, anchovies, and sardines. Fish was one of their basic foods.

War and rebellion

Europe suffered greatly from wars during the 17th century. For nearly 40 years, war ravaged Germany. In Italy one invasion followed another. In Holland and England, rebellions smoldered and escalated into war. Parts of the French countryside were continually ravaged by armies on the move, or subjected to periods of siege. Europe was tearing itself apart with muskets and cannon, and bankrupting itself with the cost of arms and fortifications.

At first, armies enlisted volunteers. In France recruiting was handled by captains who bought their office from the king. Later, "recruiting sergeants" used all kinds of tricks to persuade the young peasant men to enlist. If necessary, the sergeants would get the men drunk so that they really did not know what they were agreeing to. In some villages there was such extreme poverty that recruiters had little difficulty enlisting men. All that was necessary was to offer them decent pay. Later, when thousands of soldiers had been killed in battle, it became necessary to draft men into the army by force.

Troops on military maneuvers behaved like gangs of highwaymen. They lived off the farmers and left behind a trail of misery. When an army was forced to retreat, the soldiers burned all the crops in their path so that there would be nothing left to feed the pursuing enemy. Troops moving through the countryside meant catastrophe for the peasants.

While the soldiers made people's lives miserable by stealing and vandalizing, their own lives were far from easy. The soldiers' living conditions were very harsh. Most of the time they had to sleep in camps, sometimes in tents, and sometimes in the open. In frontier fortifications they slept half naked, packed into sordid barracks. Poorly fed and poorly paid, the soldier considered himself fortunate if he could return home with a disabled veteran's pension when he was no longer able to fight. Many men returning home after 20 or 30 years of service were astonished by the poor reception they received— but to a peasant, a soldier was just a bandit in uniform.

Soldiers attacking a farm

The Spanish brutally repressed rebellions in the Netherlands. Above, Spanish soldiers are beheading rebels. Uprisings in the Flemish towns of Antwerp, Bruges, and Ostend were supressed with equal force.

During the Thirty Years War, Germany experienced one of the harshest periods of its history. Soldiers robbed and killed everywhere. Military officers forcibly drafted peasants into the army, while in the villages their families were dying of hunger.

In Naples, Spanish domination lasted a long time, but the city's 280,000 people became more and more restless. Popular rebellions finally broke out, notably in 1647, and the ensuing repression was harsh and merciless.

The Mudejars in the south of Spain were Moslems who had been converted to Christianity by force. They were expelled by the Catholics at the beginning of the 17th century. Religious intolerance resulted in the exile of 450,000 people.

In order to weaken an enemy considered to be very rich, the French formed an alliance with the English and the Swedes to wage war against Holland. With 160,000 men commanded by Turenne, Condé, Luxembourg, and Vauban, the great French military leaders of the time, the invading armies entered Holland and took Utrecht. The Dutch employed their ultimate weapon—they opened the dikes. Water covered the country, Holland became an invincible island surrounded by water, and the invaders withdrew.

Travel by land and sea

Large coaches drawn by teams of six horses provided transportation between European cities. Service was irregular, and connections were often difficult. Most roads were hardly more than dirt paths. Traveling on them was made unpleasant and difficult by either mud or dust, depending on the season. It was sometimes easier to cross the fields than travel on the roads. In addition to the hazards of the roads themselves, travelers often had to deal with bandits who preyed upon them. When the king of France wanted to visit a neighboring city, he was often preceded by a crew of workmen who prepared the road for his passage. There were few bridges, and one had to wade or use a ferryboat to cross rivers. The abolition of forced labor in western Europe was partially responsible for the poor condition of the roads.

In order to develop faster and more dependable river transportation, the Dutch and the English built more canals. The French also improved their waterways and built the Canal du Midi. Wheat from the north traveled to Paris on boats by way of the Oise River, and then down the Seine.

Sea trade made unprecedented progress. On the Atlantic coast and the North Sea, large and small ports alike grew and prospered. The ports of Nantes, Rouen, and Saint-Malo grew to accommodate increased amounts of trade with America and China. The English and French fleets were now close on the heels of the Dutch fleet, which had once totally dominated the seas.

Enormous cargoes of wheat, herring, wood from the north, and products of the tropics were brought into Amsterdam. Along with Antwerp and London, Amsterdam became a major port of redistribution.

In spite of the hazards caused by storms and pirates, waterways were still faster and safer than roadways. Ships could carry much more merchandise than the mule convoys. The future of major trade lay in the seas.

A ship under construction in a Dutch shipyard

Streets were muddy in winter, dusty in summer, and rarely paved. Some though, were paved with what in France were called "the king's cobblestones." These were cubes of sandstone that were placed on a bed of cement and then tamped down by hand.

This English engineer traveled through Europe, mainly in the mountainous areas, in search of deposits of iron, copper, or other valuable metals. In order to cross Mont Cenis, he cleverly solved the transportation problem by using a rustic sedan chair.

Road conditions were so poor in Europe that waterways were used most of the time. When Louis XIII and Cardinal Richelieu returned to Paris from the Languedoc region, it took two weeks and dozens of horses for them to go from Tarascon to Lyons. The Loire, the Seine, and many other rivers were cluttered with boats providing regular transportation of cargo and passengers. In cities, such as Paris, London, and Amsterdam, passenger barge service existed.

Coaches were suspended on springs and sometimes had glass windows that protected passengers from the dust of the road. Liverymen were stationed at the rear. The small front wheels enabled coaches to turn in the narrow streets of cities.

In Russia during the winter, sleighs replaced coaches. Some were sumptuously decorated. The czarina's comfortable sleigh was enclosed. Inside, hot-water bottles helped fight against the cold, and thick windows kept out the snow.

Battles at sea

The Dutch had the first shipyards in Europe. But under Richelieu and Colbert, the French built up their own powerful fleet. The English allocated half their national budget to developing their splendid navy. The era of great naval battles was about to begin.

The sea-going vessels, decorated with wooden sculptures painted or gilded like church statues, cost a fortune to build. On board, superior officers had magnificent cabins inlaid with fine woods such as ebony or mahogany.

These large ships were difficult to control. Knowledge of currents, wind speed, and water depth was very important. Even under the best conditions, it might take several days of maneuvering to enter a port. The huge ships were fragile despite their size, and the commanders often feared damaging and disabling them.

On board the ships, the officers tolerated no errors or weakness from their crew. Sailors were recruited from coastal towns and trained in navigation as well as in armed combat. They endured iron discipline, and blindly obeyed their officers for fear of corporal punishment. Men in both the French and English navies were often punished by whipping. Sailors who smoked in the holds or stole drinking water were bound to the mainmast and lashed with tarred ropes.

At the start of a battle, squadrons of ships passed one after the other and bombarded the enemy. Then, as the ships drew closer together, the men fired pistols and muskets at their opponents. Finally it was time for boarding. Grappling hooks grasped the enemy's ship to pull it closer, and the men rushed on board to attack. The hand-to-hand combat was bloody and exhausting. When a ship was taken, the victors immediately lowered the enemy flag and ran up their own. The men on the losing side were taken prisoner and thrown into the hold with their ankles shackled. Only the officers received favorable treatment.

A battle between the English and Dutch fleets

An English fleet has just shelled the town of Camaret in Brittany, destroying the church belfry. From the ramparts of their fort, the townspeople, angry at the damage to their church, are firing cannon to drive the enemy away.

This galley was called l'Heureuse (The Happy One). On board, 255 prisoners were chained to their benches as rowers. To pick up the pace, the overseers whipped the rowers. If these galley slaves tried to escape, they had their nose or ears cut off.

This frigate, the Couronne, was launched in 1630. It was 48 meters long and 15 meters wide and had 3 masts and 3 decks. It was designed for squadron fighting and maintained a crew of 800 men. The hold contained fresh drinking water, ammunition for the cannons

Pirates were everywhere but particularly in the Caribbean. Working exclusively for their own profit, they attacked any vessel that came within their reach. Here they have captured an English ship and cruelly hung the sailors from the yards by their feet.

(cannonballs and barrels of powder), rope, and spare sails. Sailors found guilty of insubordination were thrown into the bottom of the hold, with shackles around their ankles, and fed only bread and water.

Bandits, plunderers ... or soldiers?

At least one million Europeans were in uniform. By the end of the century France alone maintained a force of 360,000 men. Of these, 200,000 were in the infantry. Many foreigners—German, Irish, and Swiss—were included in the French forces. The rest were more or less voluntary recruits. Increasing the size of one's troops was the general rule. The Dutch maintained a force of well-paid troops. England mobilized. Spain maintained the largest infantry. The Brandenburg elector had a superbly trained army of 25,000 men. The Russian czar placed his army under the command of experienced German instructors.

The recruitment, training, and maintainance of vast numbers of troops created problems that the states had never faced before. These problems encouraged the growth of mercenary armies. Wealthy men would recruit, equip, train, and command their own army, and sell its services to the state that offered them the most money. A well-known mercenary was Albrecht van Wallenstein whose army fought in the Thirty Years War.

Soldiers often enlisted in the army to escape from overcrowded villages. Others were lured by a taste for plundering or adventure. Often poorly paid and always badly fed, many deserted, even though they were threatened with exile or forced labor as galley slaves. However, as soon as a deserter was caught, he was often drafted once again. Armies needed men so badly, they filled their ranks in any way they could. In the French provinces, vagabonds and beggars were rounded up and turned over to recruiting sergeants!

Soldiers were sometimes proud of their uniforms. The Marquis de Louvois, minister of war under Louis XIV, dressed the French guards in blue, the queen's regiments in red, and the other troops in gray-white. The infantry wore black hats and buckled shoes, and the dashing cavalry wore magnificent cloaks.

A detachment of Russian cossacks on the march

Soldiers lived off the people. When their own food supplies ran out, the soldiers helped themselves to whatever they wanted. Since many of them had been farmers, the soldiers knew how to use a scythe and could cut the wheat and rye themselves.

Cavalry regiments were formed in France and Germany. The army purchased the best horses for these select troops. In the various schools for training officers, riding masters taught the gentlemen cadets to ride well.

Payday for soldiers in the Netherlands. Pay scales varied greatly from one army to another. In France a colonel might earn £6,000 and a second lieutenant 1,000. A simple soldier might be paid only five cents a day, out of which the army kept two cents for his board.

Young cavalry cadets were often undisciplined and responded arrogantly to orders from the old sergeants. But discipline had to prevail, so this young cavalryman is being forced to stand for hours with his foot on a stake and a flag in his hand.

Prisoners were often drafted into the infantry, and punishment for insubordination could be extremely severe—more so than in the cavalry. Below, soldiers with heavy weights attached to their ankles are being publicly punished in the village square.

The art of war

The influence of new weapons transformed the art of war. Cannons, grenades, and muskets became an essential part of military tactics. The king of Sweden, Gustavus Adolphus, was the first to recognize the importance of artillery.

Armies began to maneuver more flexibly and scientifically. Rather than one large army converging upon a single point in enemy territory, armies were divided into smaller units, which converged upon the enemy from several different points. Turenne, one of the century's finest military strategists, taught the French army how to deploy itself over an area of 100 kilometers so that no unit would interfere with another's movements. In order to succeed at this, strategies had to be planned right down to the most minute detail. Orders had to be clear, concise, and rigorously carried out to the letter. As warfare became more skillful, the discipline of the troops gained more and more importance.

The queen of the battle was unquestionably the artillery, which compelled opponents to protect themselves within fortifications of a new design. The foremost fort builder of the time was Vauban, a Frenchman who designed fortifications to take advantage of the new weapons and strategies. The complicated geometric layouts of Vauban's forts increased the range of the cannons within. A fort always had double walls with staggered towers and curved recesses. The entire structure was shaped like a massive, impenetrable star. Many times Vauban's forts were responsible for saving France from invasion.

Advances in the design of artillery enabled the infantry to fight battles throughout the countryside without being encumbered by the heavy bronze cannons that were awkward to maneuver and took a long time to set up. Early muskets were also difficult weapons to use. They were hard to aim and time-consuming to reload. However, beginning in 1670, foot soldiers were equipped with lightweight flintlock muskets that could fire up to six shots in a minute, and the cavalry began to carry short-barreled firearms. These offensive weapons transformed battle strategy. Battle tactics changed, with mobility and speed gaining new importance.

A fort under siege

Some units owned windmills and were able to produce their own wheat in the regions where they were quartered. Special units were sometimes assigned to acquiring grain supplies. Most of the time, it was taken right from the farmer's field or out of the granaries. The army did not need to purchase its food; it simply helped itself to whatever was needed.

In England a grenadier company was part of each infantry battalion. Hand grenades were little bombs thrown by soldiers called grenadiers. Grenadiers wore pointed hats, which were more practical than wide-brimmed hats when throwing grenades.

The bayonet was used in close combat beginning in 1647. The weapon is said to have been invented by the defenders of Bayonne around 1640 when, running out of ammunition, they fastened daggers at the ends of their muskets to fight off the enemy.

Swedish and Prussian armies were well equipped and well disciplined. Arms handling was gaining new importance. Soldiers needed to know how to advance in ranks and how to set themselves up in firing positions. The new weapons changed military tactics.

Musketeers were an important part of all the great European armies. They were either horse soldiers or foot soldiers who were armed with muskets. From left to right you see French, Dutch, German, and English musketeers.

Absolute monarchs and parliaments

The great powers of Europe were in the process of forming. The conquests and acquisitions of Louis XIV made France, in spite of some setbacks, nearly what it is today. The Union Act of 1707 united England and Scotland under one monarch and one Parliament. Beginning in 1640 Portugal was no longer part of Spain, and in 1648 Spain was forced to recognize the independence of the United Provinces (Holland and Belgium today).

The kings of Denmark and Poland were subject to the influence of their dangerous neighbors Gustavus Adolphus, the powerful Swedish king; Frederick William, the Great Brandenburg Elector; and Peter the Great, czar of Russia. Northern and eastern Europe were in a state of turmoil while these rulers struggled for power.

In central Europe the Habsburg monarchy, under Leopold I, ruled over Austria, Hungary, and Bohemia. For years, Austria was plagued by attacks from the Turks in the east. With help from the Polish king, and other allies, the Turks were repelled in 1697.

At this time, Italy was made up of many small states—Venice, Savoy, the Papal states, the kingdom of Naples, and several other cities and principalities. These small states were easy prey for the more powerful nations of Europe.

In England the middle class and the nobles forced the absolutist regime to grant them liberal privileges. England had a Parliament that was supposed to limit the powers of the king. In France and Spain, on the other hand, the monarchies grew stronger. The kings suppressed both the nobles' attempts at independence and the liberal tendencies of the middle classes. The accepted political model was an efficient state with a profitable tax system and many administrators working for a government whose goal was to develop by any means its financial, economic, military, and maritime power. Europe entered into a time of intense international rivalries spurred on by a merciless battle for world domination.

The nobility bows before Louis XIV, the Sun King.

The English Parliament was composed of two houses—the House of Lords, whose members represented the clergy and the nobility, and the House of Commons, whose members were elected by landholders and the middle classes. Elections were animated events.

Westerners looked toward Russia. Russia had undertaken the conquest of Siberia and since the 16th century the Russian monarch had called himself Czar (from the Latin word *Caesar*). Here the czar is receiving ambassadors of the western powers.

In the Republic of the United Provinces, each province had an assembly, a secretary, and a governor. Elected deputies from each province attended the assembly of the States General in the Hague. Above them hung flags captured from Spanish armies.

The Josselin castle in Brittany belonged to the great lords of Rohan. During the reign of Louis XIII, the Catholic noblemen, like the Protestants, were opposed to the politics of Cardinal Richelieu.

Richelieu would not tolerate the nobility's opposition to the royal power, and he was responsible for the destruction of numerous castles. In 1629 the Josselin castle was shelled by order of the king.

One king, one faith, one law

In England and France the power of the monarchy was in question. The English struggled fiercely to maintain the rights of their Parliament and to prevent their king, Charles I, from levying taxes without parliamentary approval. The disputes between the king and Parliament went on for 18 years, and in 1642 culminated in England's first civil war. The aristocracy supported Charles and the monarchy, while the merchants and smaller landowners were opposed to an absolute monarchy and sided with Parliament. Another issue of the war was religion. The king and his supporters favored the Church of England, while their opponents belonged to Presbyterian or Puritan congregations.

The king's dashing forces were called Cavaliers. His opponents, led by Oliver Cromwell, were called Roundheads because of their haircuts. In 1648 Cromwell's army defeated the king's forces, and Cromwell was named Lord Protector. He ruled until his death in 1658, when Charles II, son of Charles I, was brought back from exile in France and installed on the throne. In 1685 Charles II died and was suceeded by his brother, James II. During James' short and disastrous reign new rebellions broke out against his absolutist regime, leading to a compromise that made England the first parliamentary monarchy in Europe.

In France, members of the French parliament and the middle classes united with the nobility and upper classes to protest the royal power and to fight against the government in a series of rebellions. Meanwhile, Cardinal Richelieu, and later Mazarin, ran France for the young king, Louis XIV. When Mazarin died in 1661, the twenty-three-year-old Louis took over the running of France himself. He reestablished the authority of the monarchy, resumed the fight with the other great powers for domination of Europe, and formed his government with officials of his own choice. In France "absolutism" was the answer to English "parliamentarism."

Combat between Cromwell's Roundheads and the Cavaliers of Charles I

In order to resist invasion from the Muslim Turks, the embattled Christians of Cyprus allied themselves to the powerful city-state of Venice. However, all defense efforts failed and the war-torn island was finally ceded to the Turks.

After his vain attempts to impose absolute power, Charles I of England was defeated by Cromwell and his army. Captured, tried for treason, and condemned to death, the king was executed in 1649. The English refused to tolerate an all-powerful monarch.

In 1648 rebellion broke out in Paris. Members of the parliament, emulating their counterparts in England, attempted to prevent the crown from levying taxes. The powerful Cardinal Mazarin ordered the arrest of several rebellious princes, and all of Paris rose up in arms. By

January, 1649, the rebellion became so severe that the queen left the city, and Mazarin himself fled in 1651. However, royal troops succeeded in retaking the city, and in February, 1653, Mazarin returned in triumph; the rebellion against the crown was over.

In Prague civil war began in 1618 when, angered because of persecution by the Catholic Hapsburg monarchy, a group of Protestants threw three imperial officials from a window. They fell 15 meters but landed unharmed in a heap of rubbish.

In 1640 the nobility and clergy led Portugal in a revolt against Spain. In Lisbon, citizens invaded the palace of a Portuguese agent of the Spanish rulers and killed him. Years of unrest followed, and Portugal became officially independent of Spain in 1668.

Churches—warriors and missionaries

After the ordeal of the Protestant Reformation, the Catholic Church set out to reconquer Europe. From their pulpits, preachers stormed, threatened, and enflamed their congregations; in some areas inciting them to wild, almost fanatical reaction. In Nice, Italy, a Catholic missionary had pyres built, onto which women were exhorted to throw their costly jewelry and other worldly objects to be consumed by flames. Flagellants, people who whipped themselves as a religious penance, wandered through the streets, wearing crowns of thorns, their shoulders covered with blood.

France, Spain, and Austria became uncompromising in their devotion to Catholicism. Religious dissension was not allowed; those who resisted suffered. Richelieu destroyed Protestant strongholds and had certain well-known leaders beheaded. In 1685 Louis XIV revoked the Edict of Nantes, which had granted religious freedom to the Huguenots, Protestants who were among France's most industrious citizens. They contributed greatly to the economy as skilled craftsmen, successful merchants and financiers, and well-educated middle-class citizens. They eventually left France and took their skills to the Protestant countries of England, Holland, and Brandenburg. French industry and ultimately the French economy suffered from their loss.

In Germany the Thirty Years War began as a religious war. The Protestant princes formed the Protestant Union to protect themselves against the papacy, the Hapsburgs, and the Bavarian princes of the Catholic League. In England Cromwell's Puritans accused the Church of England of papism and religious weakness.

However, religion was not limited to political struggle. The Church worked hard to relieve some of the terrible miseries of the poverty that plagued both cities and countryside. The injustices were so appalling that charity became a moral obligation and missionary orders attacked all forms of poverty. This work was in the end actually the most effective possible form of Catholic reconquest.

A Spanish priest preaches in a beautiful baroque church.

The Russian Orthodox funeral rites (shown above) resembled those of the Greeks. Offerings were placed on the tombs and in the coffins. Before closing the coffin, a piece of bread and a glass of beer or mead was placed inside.

The Dutch, who for the most part were Protestants, created a land of freedom and refuge in Holland. They welcomed Jews, did not persecute Catholics, and at the same time faithfully practiced their reformed religion in their simple churches.

Slavery persisted on the shores of the Mediterranean and pirates from north Africa kidnapped many Christians from the western coasts. Religious orders, such as the Knights of Malta, gathered the financial means necessary to ransom the captives.

Two hundred thousand Protestants fled from France when the Edict of Nantes was revoked by Louis XIV. Rather than convert, they preferred to go into exile in Protestant countries. The king's devotion to Catholicism led to the country's loss of many valuable citizens.

Inspired by the benevolent acts of St. Vincent de Paul, ladies of French society practiced charity by visiting the poor and ministering to the sick. However, these "daughters of charity" mainly prayed for their souls, leaving the more humble tasks to their servants.

Europe's nobility tamed

Louis XIV traveled through the huge park of Versailles in a curious-looking old-fashioned carriage drawn by footmen. Enthroned on this strange vehicle, the king was surrounded by his courtiers, the nobles of his court. In the royal palace, everyone had a particular function, defined by strict court etiquette. The most famous people in France felt privileged to become food officers or masters of the robes. To be appointed the king's chamberlain or first gentleman of the chamber was a most distinguished favor. Living in the palace at Versailles was a great honor. Many aristocrats abandoned their own beautiful palaces to seek humble accommodations at Versailles, which housed over 10,000 people including soldiers and servants.

The French aristocracy was now entirely controlled by Louis XIV. The tamed nobles no longer rebelled against the king but plotted to obtain favors from him. However, the king was hardly generous with his favors, and when he did bestow them, it was with grudging condescension. Women also participated in the intrigues of the court. They were continually vying with each other for recognition and prestige. Families who had been friends and allies for years, now fought with each other over a trifling favor from the king.

The French court was not the only one of its kind in Europe. It became a model, and the etiquette of Versailles spread to Austria, Prussia, and later on, to Russia.

On the whole, the European governments were taking political control out of the hands of the nobles. Even in England, many of the lords grew tired of the struggle and settled into their large castles and estates to devote themselves to hunting and farming. However, though the nobility was losing power all over Europe, they still possessed their main source of wealth—land.

The nobility of France, Germany, and Spain had plenty to do outside of life at court. Their kings led them into wars and entrusted them with the command of regiments and companies. This time they went to war for the sake of the state rather than to defend the interests of their own class.

Louis XIV and his court in the park at Versailles

Under Louis XIII dueling was the rage in France. The nobles, not yet domesticated by the customs of the court of Louis XIV, fought for love as well as over political or religious matters. Richelieu finally forbade dueling and punished disobedience with death in some cases. Poor young men arriving in Paris from the country counted on their swords to make their way. They enlisted in one of the companies of guardsmen attached to king, cardinal, or prince; some, perhaps, became musketeers.

Billiards was very popular in England, and its popularity soon spread to other parts of Europe. Louis XIV enjoyed it, and ladies liked to play and bet on the game. At the time, the cue sticks were shorter with a curved end, and the game was played with a pin and a hoop.

A hairdresser has delivered a full-bottomed wig to this lord. Assistants to the wigmaker freshen up the curly wig that cost a fortune. Under his wig, the lord's head is shaven. The most sought-after wigs were ash-gray.

In Holland and Italy the wealthy, including kings and princes, bought pieces of art to add to their collections. They also were very interested in scientific instruments. Some people owned valuable private natural-history collections.

Hunting was still a lordly pastime. In Europe, people already used rifles to hunt big game. These were loaded by the barrel and were quite different from muskets. A flint set the powder on fire, and there was no need to light a wick.

The arts at court

At a royal court artists often shared the same position as the court buffoons, barbers, and astrologers. In Spain the name of the famous painter Velasquez appeared on court personnel records. He was dressed at the king's expense and performed various duties for the court. At the bullfights, his place was in the fourth row with the chambermaids. He painted pictures of the royal family and court buffoons, but was also expected to do his job as a courtier. Velasquez served the crown as a gentleman of the king's bedchamber, an assistant superintendent of works, and finally as chamberlain to the king.

The Velasquez painting below is called *Las Meninas*. It shows the young Spanish princess and several members of the royal household. Reflected in the mirror at the center are King Philip IV and his queen. At the left is Velasquez. After the painting was completed, Velasquez was named to the Order of the Knights of Santiago. According to legend, King Philip IV then added the red cross of the Knights of Santiago to Velasquez's chest on the painting as pictured below. However, it is more likely that Velasquez himself made the addition.

An artist's or author's situation was rather shaky. While Louis XIV of France granted pensions to writers Racine and Corneille and defended Molière against his enemies, he banished others who refused to become part of his retinue. The famous sculptor Bernini answered to the pope, and the playwright Lope de Vega received a salary from the duke of Alba.

Some artists like Reubens, who lived sumptuously at the expense of the archduke of Austria, became very wealthy. Reubens collected all kinds of treasures in his house in Antwerp—paintings by Raphael, da Vinci, Tintoretto, and Titian. When he died in 1640 he owned several houses, land, and farms, and he had just purchased a castle. During the same time, a humble painter like Georges de la Tour received only a small fee for each canvas he painted for the duke of Lorraine. There were many impoverished artists for each financial success. For every artist showered with honors, there were many who lived no better than servants.

The king of Spain, so the legend goes, painted the cross of the Knights of Santiago on Velasquez's chest in the painting called *Las Meninas*.

On the grounds of castles and estates throughout Europe, landscape architects designed beautiful and elaborate parks, lawns, flower beds, and shrubbery. Lakes, fountains, and statues were also included. At Versailles, the gardens came close to perfection.

Theater was very popular everywhere and playwrights wrote hundreds of plays. As you can see from the picture above, the stage was not separated from the audience by an orchestra pit. The nobles sat on chairs, and the general public stood to watch performances.

Many great sculptors like Bernini came from Italy. Bernini made this statue of Pope Urban VIII and in Rome he also created a number of fountains and baroque facades. In St. Peter's basilica he sculpted St. Peter's pulpit and the wreathed columns of the baldachino.

At Versailles the king built the Grand Trianon as a retreat. The park at Versailles was especially beautiful. The king used the various groves of the park to entertain his court. In addition to dinners and suppers, open-air theater also delighted the king and his court.

Writers already enjoyed meeting together even before the French Academy was founded by Richelieu. The literary world was a lively, warm, and free environment, but many of the freethinking writers were not accepted by the authorities.

Families and children

In wealthy families, the children were usually quite fortunate. They lived in clean, well-kept houses, were well fed, and wore shining clogs and beautiful clothes. They washed with warm water from clean wooden buckets and played with broomstick horses, quoits, cup-and-ball games, dolls, and balls. Some babies were sumptuously dressed and, beginning at the age of five, some young nobles even carried a small sword.

The upper classes in the towns and cities gave their children every attention. Healthy wet nurses from the country came to town to nurse the babies born to rich families. These fortunate children stood a better chance of reaching adulthood than many 17th-century children.

On the other hand, conditions among the poor peasants of the countryside were tragic. The average woman gave birth to many children and tried to raise them the best she could. But the care was woefully inadequate and before reaching the age of one year, nearly half the babies born in the 17th century died. Many were victims of malnutrition and famine. Children as well as adults contracted terrible diseases, such as dysentery, smallpox, and fevers, which were incurable at the time. The average life expectancy was about twenty-two years, although the wealthy could expect to live quite a bit longer than the poor peasants.

The children of the poor began to work at the age of eight or ten. They were frequently placed in the homes of somewhat better-off farmers who fed them in return for their work. When there was no work, they wandered from village to village in search of employment.

In spite of everything, marriages and births among the poor were numerous, and the struggle to survive and carry on from generation to generation was constant and determined. If it were not for the unquenchable vitality of these peasant families, war, epidemics, and famine might have triumphed over the population of Europe.

The well-kept home of a wealthy Dutch family

In some noble families, only the older sons could remain on the family's land. Younger sons had to leave. When they were of an age to seek their fortune, their father would give them a sum of money and a letter of recommendation to a great lord.

The birth rate in Europe was high. Some families had ten children or more. It was difficult for a mother to care for them all. In England, a clever device called a "baby-trot" was invented. The baby was restrained by a rod that pivoted around an axle.

There weren't enough doctors in the cities, and none at all in the countryside. Babies were delivered by midwives or experienced neighbors. A lack of hygiene caused many fatalities. In Catholic families, a newborn child was immediately baptized.

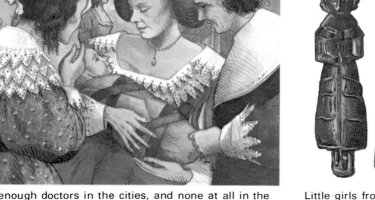

Little girls from rich families owned beautifully made and dressed wooden dolls. Nothing was too good for them. The cardinal of La Valette gave a little girl of the Bourbon family a doll with her own room and clothes valued at $2500!

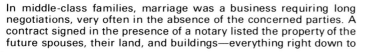

In middle-class families, marriage was a business requiring long negotiations, very often in the absence of the concerned parties. A contract signed in the presence of a notary listed the property of the future spouses, their land, and buildings—everything right down to

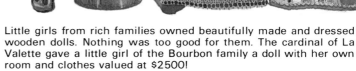

the sheets! Marriage was also a means of climbing the social ladder. A middle-class man did not hesitate to give his daughter an attractive dowry if she married a noble, even if the noble was impoverished. This gave the noble a chance to rehabilitate his finances.

Parish schools and universities

In 1690 more than 75 percent of the men and 90 percent of the women of France were illiterate. The proportion was still greater in Italy, Spain, and Germany. To combat this state of affairs, the Protestant countries as well as the Catholic kingdoms began to develop schools and send their children to them. Each country wanted to inculcate the state religion. In Protestant Holland, schools taught Calvin's doctrine. In Catholic France, Louis XIV recommended the opening of Catholic "junior schools" in each parish, especially in the Protestant regions, where entire families were forcefully converted. The bishops placed the greatest importance on increasing the number of schools—toward the end of the 17th century, in the 1,159 parishes of Normandy, there were 1,161 schools, including 306 for girls. At that time, many Protestants lived in that region. In Paris there were more than 300 schools, all Catholic. In Lyons there were 16 Catholic free schools for poor children.

Country preachers or their assistants served as schoolmasters in the parish schools. These men were often very ignorant, and most of the time they had another profession. A teacher might also be a cooper (a man who makes and repairs wooden tubs and casks), a clock maker, or a wine maker. The schoolmasters' main concern was to get their pupils to read the catechism that prepared them for their Communion. Moreover, they were far from having all the village children in their classes, since starting at eight years of age, most of the children went to the fields to tend the flocks.

Few children, consequently, were able to pursue their studies. Those privileged ones entered sixth grade at age fourteen and took their baccalaureate degree four years later. Then they attended a university, where they obtained a more advanced degree or even a doctorate. The most learned ones often completed their studies at age twenty-five, but these were the elite, who were generally destined for careers in religion.

A young woman plays the spinet at a family concert in Delft.

Bookstores, such as this one in England, were frequented by people who sometimes assembled superb library collections. French collectors came to England and Holland, where they could acquire works forbidden at home for political or religious reasons.

The inhabitants of the French countryside, illiterate for the most part, required the services of a public writer when they needed to write a letter. The latter traveled from village to village to serve his clients. Only the clergy could dispense with this help.

The most famous university in Protestant Europe was the one at Leyden, created in Holland by William of Orange. Doctors of theology trained not only the students who would become pastors, but also future scientists, lawyers, and philologists.

A slate, an hourglass, a goose-feather pen, and an inkwell—that was enough equipment for an evening school in Protestant Holland, where children and at times adults came to learn how to read. The desire to learn spread through the less privileged social classes. School was not obligatory nor was it usually free, even for poor children. The rich, however, hired private tutors.

Science, an international language

In the 17th century, modern thought upset custom and roused indignation among established scholars. In 1633 the judges of the Holy Office condemned Galileo for having dared assert that the earth turned. A few years before that, in Pisa, he had established the law of falling bodies: equal weights—a kilogram of lead and a kilogram of feathers—fall at the same speed. Until then this phenomenon had never been observed.

This discovery, like the discovery of atmospheric pressure and that of universal gravitation, had profound repercussions. The infinitely small and the infinitely large were no longer the object of the philosophers' speculation. They were instead now open to rational investigation by men of science. Pascal conversed with the mathematician Fermat, Galileo with the astronomer Kepler. The private academies of Europe began in Italy with the founding of the Academia dei Lincei to which Galileo belonged. In Holland, safe from the Inquisition and the traditional scholars of the Sorbonne, Descartes became interested in scientific research with Isaac Beeckmann. Private academies existed in France—in Caen; in Rouen; in Toulouse, where Fermat worked; in Aix-en-Provence, where the great scientist de Peiresc reigned; and in Clermont-Ferrand, where Pascal worked. England, with Isaac Newton and Robert Hooke, had scientists who were also mathematicians, physicists, philosophers, experimenters, and astronomers. And at the beginning of the century, in Denmark, Tycho Brahe founded a new astronomy based on observation.

The rich, fashionable, and powerful encouraged and protected science. The French cardinal and statesman Mazarin introduced the Italian scientists to France. Descartes was the guest of Queen Christina of Sweden. In the royal or princely courts, researchers often found support against the censorship of religion. If scientists were persecuted in their own country, they easily found refuge in the private universities of Holland or Germany. During this period, science knew no political boundaries.

The residents of Pisa comment on Galileo's experiments.

Studies on atmospheric pressure increased in Europe after the discoveries of the Italian physicist Torricelli. A German, Otto von Guericke, thought of testing the pressure of the atmosphere by a unique experiment. After creating a vacuum in two close-fitting hemispheres, he harnessed eight horses to each of the two hemispheres. They were unable to separate them, yet the hemispheres fell apart when air was let in through a valve. This experiment took place in Magdebourg in 1654.

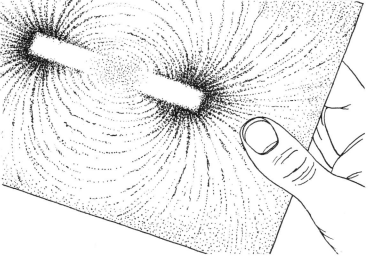

The lines of force in a magnetic field were shown by iron filings dusted onto a thin piece of cardboard placed over a bar magnet. In this way the mysterious magnetic forces were made visible for the first time.

Known since antiquity, antimony is a solid substance, silver-white, easy to crush, and often used in medicine. In the 17th century miraculous properties were attributed to it. The man is heating antimony with a lens to change its form.

Pascal launched an expedition to Puy de Dôme to verify his theory on atmospheric pressure. His brother-in-law measured the pressure on the mercury column at the bottom of the mountain and then carried the barometer to the top and measured the pressure there.

Maps of the moon became more and more precise, due to astronomers' observations. The early maps were published by the most famous engravers. Here one of them, Claude Mellan, shows in fine detail the various mountains of the moon.

Doctors, surgeons, and medicine

The plague afflicted London. Dogs suspected of transmitting the terrible disease were all killed. Diseased people battling against death saw their door marked with a cross, symbolically blocking up their house. They were even forced to receive food through a window. But in spite of these precautions, thousands of people died.

In Toulouse, France, when the plague struck, the parliament deserted the city for several months. People prayed continually in the hope that their prayers would help to drive off the curse of the plague. Certainly there was little doctors could do to help the sick and dying. Many doctors, fearing for their own lives, fled to the relative safety of the countryside. People who died on the streets were carried away in carts by gravediggers, and buried in common graves.

In summer, in addition to the plague, dysentery ravaged the land, while destructive fevers also killed great numbers of people. Cures were nonexistent, and the lack of proper hygiene intensified the problems. Doctors regularly used bleedings and enemas as remedies. The only other option they had at their disposal were a few drugs whose effects were not well known. The discovery of quinine helped to reduce the lingering effects of some fevers. But man's inability to combat disease made his life short and precarious. Average life expectancy was about twenty-two years. Many children were born only to die before their first birthday. Babies were delivered by people who were completely ignorant of the process of childbirth. They often crippled unfortunate babies who presented themselves in difficult positions during delivery. Due to the lack of cleanliness, mothers sometimes died from infections. There were few doctors and surgeons, and their knowledge was extremely limited. Also they had little means of expanding their meager knowledge. Surgery was still quite primitive and risky. Doctors had no means of preventing infection and no form of anesthesia. To a patient an operation was an intolerable form of torture only slightly more attractive than death.

The plague ravaged London.

Hygiene was nonexistent among rural families. In country dwellings, doors were made of sod and an entire household might sleep in the same bed. Lice were a common problem. There were no drugs to eliminate parasites and people deloused themselves in groups.

Doctors, still very unskilled, bled their patients in an effort to drop temperatures. To try to cure a stomachache, purges were sold by the apothecaries. When these were ineffective, doctors administered enemas.

Important citizens were responsible for the administration of city hospitals. A person who wished to be a municipal judge had to spend time taking care of hospitals that welcomed the needy as well as the sick. With the help of monks and nuns, upper-class women attended

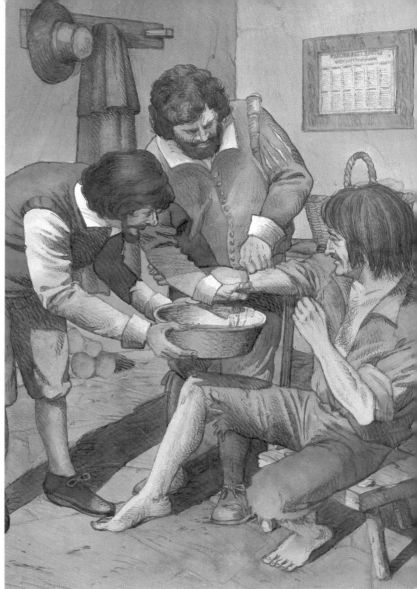

For most physicians, bleedings were a universal treatment. They frequently administered them to the sick, which only served to further weaken them, and even to healthy people. It was thought that an excess of blood in the veins was the cause of many diseases.

to the patients. In time of famine, hospitals were overrun by the undernourished population who took refuge there to escape slow but certain death.

Microscopes, barometers, and chronometers

In the 17th century, scholars were just beginning to believe that scientific experiments could be as useful to the progress of thought as mathematical reasoning. And the development of experimentation went hand in hand with the development of scientific instruments—thermometers, barometers, clocks, and lenses for telescopes and microscopes. In 1610 Johannes Fabricius of Germany saw sunspots through a smoked-glass telescope. The Italians and the Dutch became masters in the art of grinding lenses. Galileo and Torricelli made their own telescopes. Christian Huygens of Holland developed new methods of grinding and polishing lenses and built better telescopes than had been available. Robert Hooke of England greatly improved the compound microscope and used it to further the science of biology. Skilled craftsmen in both Holland and Italy began to build microscopes. In England, for about six pounds, one could buy a compound microscope. This was a microscope with two lenses with which precise investigations could be performed.

The measurement of temperature also fascinated scientists. However, a hundred years would pass before the thermometer would become a really accurate instrument. As for the barometer, it aroused real enthusiasm.

This search for precision was also applied to the measurement of time. Huygens was the first to use the compound pendulum to regulate clocks. This innovation permitted the building of remarkably precise chronometers.

Thus, thanks to the desire of men to measure time and heat and to explore the unknown worlds of the heavens and the cell, science was endowed with essential instruments. These would assure the continued development of the fascinating experimental sciences that before that time had been in their infancy—physics, chemistry, physiology, and anatomy.

Scientists develop the first thermometers.

We do not know which of two Dutchmen, Zacharias Janssen or Cornelis Drebbel, invented the microscope. Nevertheless, the instrument was constantly improved thereafter—the laws of optics were applied as quickly as they were discovered.

Johannes Hevelius of Germany studied sunspots, discovered the librations of the moon (periodic alternations in the visibility of its parts), and published a detailed map of the moon's surface. The giant telescope shown was constructed in 1670 to advance his discoveries.

The French Pascal invented a type of calculator. Completed in 1645, his invention used a system of drums and notched wheels to perform addition and subtraction. The mechanization was done through a rather complex system that functioned by gravity.

Torricelli invented the barometer, in which he used a tube of mercury to balance the weight of the atmosphere. With it, changes in atmospheric pressure could be measured. Torricelli was a scribe for Galileo, who had become blind, and an ingenious experimenter.

Europeans in China and the Americas

In the 17th century, one person in six was European.
But the Europeans were everywhere! Exploiting their knowledge of navigation to the maximum, they were exploring the world. Masters of the Atlantic from north to south, and of the Mediterranean Sea, they pressed onward through the Red Sea toward the Indian Ocean and the China Sea.

From the days of the Spanish and Portuguese conquests, the whites dominated South America. Lacking workers for their plantations and mines, they imported almost 12 million black slaves bought on the African coast. Toward 1700 the American Indian population was about 11 million. There were no more than 700,000 Europeans in South America, but they owned the mines that produced precious metals, as well as the best land. As for North America, it had very few inhabitants: 250,000 people lived on the 50,000 square kilometers controlled by the Europeans. The vast open plains of the interior, where several Indian tribes still roamed freely, were nearly empty.

It was in Asia that Europeans found the greatest population density. Colonists and merchants from Europe had a hard time settling on this immense continent. However, they played an increasingly active economic role in the trade in tea and spices carried on by the big English, Dutch, and French companies. Regular trading posts were established in the large centers.

The Europeans confined their exploration and trade largely to the coastal areas. Central Asia, like North America and continental China, was an almost unknown desert. The Russians explored Siberia to find, and if possible convert, nomadic tribes who lived by hunting, fishing, and raising animals. Some expeditions also headed toward the Great North.

The interior regions of Africa were totally unexplored. The Europeans, who did not dare venture along the rivers, contented themselves with establishing trading posts along the coasts, just as they did in Asia.

White overseers supervise black slaves in this sugar mill in Brazil.

In 1608 the French, led by Samuel de Champlain, founded Quebec on the site of an old Indian village. They hurried to build fortifications to protect the city not only from Indian raids but also from British attacks.

After conquering Mexico at the beginning of the 16th century, the Spanish brought many black slaves from Africa to work in the mines and on the land. Whites, blacks, and Indians thus lived side by side in the towns.

Greenland was named by the Viking Eric the Red in the 10th century, in an attempt to attract colonists from Iceland and Denmark. Eskimo settlements had existed on the frozen island for many centuries. During the 15th century, the European settlements on the southwest

The Samoyeds were Mongols who lived in northern Siberia. They could not survive without the reindeer. These animals provided them with meat, with fat to light their homes, leather to make clothes, and tendons for bowstrings.

coast disappeared, probably due to increasingly harsh climatic conditions. Systematic exploration resumed at the end of the 16th century as explorers like Hudson, Davys, and Baffin searched for a northwest passage to the Orient.

English merchants came to the ports of China to buy the tea that was becoming popular with the people of London. Here, while a merchant negotiates the price with a Chinese producer, servants pack the precious leaves into boxes.

The Garden of Animals

**(Where one can learn all
about God's creatures
and those sent by the devil.)**

1601 France

Olivier de Serres, who published a useful book entitled *Theater of Agriculture and Cultivation of the Fields,* ordered that 20,000 mulberry bushes be planted in the Tuileries Garden to feed the silkworms.

1605 France

Antoine de Pluvinel, director of the Great Stables of King Henry IV, has produced the first *carrousel,* or military tournament, ever seen in France. This talented horseman has undertaken the equestrian education of the dauphin Louis.

1605 Morocco

A traveler named Marquet, sent by Henry IV, king of France and of Navarre, said that he saw lions come and go freely in the houses of the rich lords of Morocco. He even visited a "House of Lions" where he saw a dog play with the great beasts. The lions apparently feared the dog's barks, which prevented them from quarreling. By barking, it separated them and obliged them to live peaceably.

1610 France

A traveling animal show has come to Paris and exhibited a herd of ostriches to the curious spectators. The owner of these big African birds sells feathers to the lords who desire them for plumage to trim their hats.

1611 Holy Roman Empire

In the Franche-Comté region, a tribunal has condemned Beatrice Taschez to banishment. She is the wife of Jean Jacquot, from Charriez. She was accused of catching, for the devil, a rat whose belly was as white as snow.

1611 France

In the Limousin province, the judges have heard the confessions of a priest who is guilty

of dealings with the infernal powers. Pierre Aupetit, age 50, the priest of the village of La Fossas, told of the various forms the devil can embody when he appears. At the witches' revels the devil appears as a sheep that is more black than white. When this priest visits the sick, the devil takes the shape of a big black fly and tells him what he should do. During the holy mass, the devil most often assumes the form of a butterfly and forbids him to pronounce the words of the ritual. Finally, on several occasions, Pierre Aupetit has seen the devil enter the church through the window, in the form of a black cat. Also, witnesses have declared that this demoniac priest has attended the witches' revels with pigs, which he places in a circle. They say that those pigs are able to talk to each other in French.

1612 England

Until now, nobody has ever thought of dissecting an ostrich to compare its anatomy with that of our barnyard poultry. An English doctor, William Harvey, has undertaken this operation for the first time. Nobody is familiar with the results of his observations, nor with the drawings of the parts of the body that he has made.

1615 Switzerland

In several cantons of this country, there is a belief that sometimes one finds wormlike animals in the human body that are put there by evil spirits. They may be worms, toads, frogs, or even small lizards. This is why children's navals often hide *vermis umbilicalis,* or the umbilical worm, also called Saint Guy's worm. Slowly but surely it devours them alive, unless it can be removed by attaching a live fish to the possessed child's belly. If the worm abandons the body and eats the fish, leaving nothing but the bones, then the child is saved. Also, accord-

ing to a belief based on judges' findings during numerous witch trials, there is a serpent from hell, called *furis infernalis,* which the devil is capable of dropping upon animal herds from high in the air. This evil creature pierces the animals' bellies and they die shortly after.

1627 Poland

The body of a wild female auroch has just been discovered in the forest about 50 kilometers from the city of Warsaw. This old cow was probably the last wild specimen of the species.

1628 Spain

Among the treasures lost by the Spanish fleet off Cuba was a large quantity of precious llama bezoars. These stonelike concretions are also found in the stomachs of goats from Iran, antelopes from Africa, and sometimes monkeys and porcupines. They are commonly believed to help in curing epilepsy, plague, dizziness, poisoning, and many other ailments. They are so sought after that their price is equivalent to ten times their weight in gold.

1629 Poland

Living on the property of Prince Radziwill Christopher II are twelve camels. These are quite similar to those that are kept by King Christian V of Denmark in his park in Frederics-Borg.

1631 France

An elephant exhibited in France for several years by a Dutchman called Sevender has arrived in Toulon. In 1626, in Paris, the governor of Montreuil ordered the erection of fencing around the beast, so that it could be kept longer in the city. The following year the elephant was taken to Rouen. In Toulon it has just received a visit from Fabri de

Peiresc, one of our most renowned scientists, who journeyed from Aix especially to see and weigh the animal. He carefully placed his hand inside the elephant's mouth and grasped one of its teeth to better know its shape. He could not examine the teeth without touching them since the elephant covers them with its tongue when it opens its mouth.

1636 Kingdom of Siam

Upon returning from a trip, the explorer Hodocus Schoutens, who visited this Asian country, told how surprised he was by the large number of elephants the king owned. He counted up to 6,000 beasts. One was completely white and was worshiped by the natives.

1645 Spain

With the support of King Philip IV, bullfights have become very popular in this country. Almost every Spanish city has its plaza de toros. Even in the smallest villages, these entertainments take place each Sunday and sometimes during the week. The greatest bullrings of all are those in Madrid, Valencia, and Barcelona.

1648 Sweden

A lion fight was presented before the court for the coronation festival of Queen Christina. One of the beasts was captured by Count Koenigsmarck at the time of the conquest of Prague, and was kept in Stockholm in a pit built for it near the royal palace.

1648 United Provinces

Every year at mid-Lent in Flanders and especially in Cambrai, people still follow the custom of locking up cats in iron cages and suspending them over big bonfires.

1648 Norway

At the court of King Christian IV, a child was fatally wounded by one of the palace bears. In an effort to avoid such accidents, their keeper ties the front paws of these great creatures behind their backs. But it was with its formidable jaws that the bear managed to hurt the unfortunate young child.

1650 France

In the recently published *Great Art of Artillery,* it is recommended that in order to overcome the strongholds of the enemy, a gas made from toad flesh rotted in goat manure and saltpeter should be used. The material is then burned with sulfur and coal, which gives off a creeping stench that pervades the most secret retreats of the besieged fortress.

1656 France

On April 6 a witch was burned alive in Villeneuve-de-Berg in Vivarais. She admitted having gone into houses at night, in the form of a cat, to kidnap children.

1660 Italy

The monks of the Great Saint Bernard Hospice have started to breed very large dogs to be used to guard their monastery, as well as to work in their kitchens. Chained in a large wheel, these dogs turn the spits on which the monks cook their quarters of beef or venison.

1663 France

Jean-Baptiste Colbert has decided to import Barbary stallions from north Africa to improve the quality of our horses of Normandy, which the king needs to replenish his cavalry regiments.

1668 Denmark

In Copenhagen, King Frederic III has set up a House of Lions. Several of the beasts living there consume 20 pounds of meat per day.

1668 France

The zoo of Versailles has just received an elephant, a gift from King Peter II of Portugal to King Louis XIV. The huge animal is extremely popular.

1668 Duchy of Hesse

In the very large zoo they have built at Cassel, the landgraves (counts) of Hess have two particularly rare animals, which they say are aurochs. Scientisfs say it is likely that these are descendents of those great extinct animals that have bred with domestic animals wandering in the forest. This is indicated by their coat, which is flecked with white.

1670 France

Jean-Baptiste Colbert, who has been the king's secretary of state for the past two years, ordered that two cats be put aboard each of his majesty's ships. They will fight the rats that are multiplying and ravaging the ships' provisions and cargoes.

1671 Italy

The naturalist Francesco Redi has just published the result of his studies of frog tadpoles in his book *Experiments into the Generations of Insects*. According to him, the frogs, after their transformation, leave the water in which they developed and seek refuge in cracks in the ground, under rocks, or in the grass.

1678 England

Following the decision made in 1622 by his predecessor King James I to regulate horse races on the field at Newmarket, King Charles II authorized such games to take place in every region of the kingdom. It

seems that the court and the people enjoy them very much. To improve the speed of their horses, the British have imported purebred Arabian stallions from the East. It is in the best of form to have some of these magnificent, costly horses in one's stable.

1680 France

In the book of short stories he just published, Gédéon Tallemant des Reaux describes the various tricks the numerous trained bears in Paris can perform. Vincent Voiture, who enjoys practical jokes, found two of these performers in the Rue St. Thomas du Louvre and had them secretly enter the Hôtel de Rambouillet, the famous home and literary salon of the Marquise de Rambouillet. The marquise was busy reading with her back to a screen. Hearing a noise behind the screen, Madame de Rambouillet turned around and was terrified to see two enormous faces staring at her. This prank provoked many laughs.

The bear trainers are mostly peasants from Ustou and other small villages in the county of Foix, and every spring they travel through Europe with their beasts. The animals are caught as cubs and then trained after their claws have been cut.

1681 England

A fossil head of a rhinoceros has been discovered near Canterbury.

1681 France

After thirteen years in the zoo at Versailles, the elephant given to King Louis XIV by King Peter II of Portugal has died. The Academy was immediately summoned, and Monsieur du Verney proceeded to dissect it. Monsieur Claude Perrault described the main parts and Monsieur de la Hire did the drawings. The expenses paid to Monsieur Couplet on that occasion amounted to about £104. For this operation, the animal was laid out on a stage high enough so the numerous spectators could see the work being performed by the scholars. The king himself was present for the examination of several parts of the body. Upon his arrival, he inquired about the anatomist, whom he could not see. Monsieur du Verney suddenly appeared from the animal's flanks, where he had been engulfed. His unexpected appearance greatly amused the king.

At the time of its death, it was found that the elephant, which they had always believed to be a male, was in fact a female. During its lifetime, it consumed 80 pounds of bread, 12 pints of wine, and 2 buckets of soup every single day. However, every other day, instead of soup with bread, it was given 2 buckets of biscuits with water. The beast also received an ear of corn every day, from which it ate the kernels. It used the cob to fan itself. Moreover, when it went for walks in good weather, it ate grass that it tore up with its trunk.

1682 Austria

A horrible drama took place in the Neugebaü zoo, which belongs to Emperor Leopold I. The keeper's daughter, who each day brought the lions their food and with whom they were very gentle, decided to perform this daily task on her wedding night. Since

she had not yet changed from her wedding gown, one of the beasts did not recognize her and jumped in front of the door, thus preventing her from leaving. The wedding guests came running and threw the young woman a rope, which she grasped. But the lion, goaded and furious, attacked the unfortunate soul and tore her to pieces before her friends could manage to pull her out.

1682 France

In February, in honor of the Persian ambassador who had come to greet the king on behalf of his master, a fight was organized in Vincennes between an elephant from the zoo of Versailles and a royal tiger. The latter finally died under the violent blows of the enormous pachyderm. Its corpse was brought to a nearby field, and the gentlemen from the Academy of sciences were summoned for a dissection. Prior to their arrival, the neighborhood peasants tore out the beast's whiskers, which they believed contained a violent poison.

1682 Morocco

The emperor of Morocco has sent to Paris as a gift a tamed female tiger, as gentle as a dog. The animal was brought to Saint-Germain and presented to the queen, who is enjoying it very much.

1682 Austria

The horses used by the riders of the Imperial Spanish Riding School in Vienna are highly praised. They are from the Lipizzaner breed, a name that was given to them because of their place of origin. In 1580 the archduke Charles, son of Emperor Ferdinand I decided to create a center for breeding quality horses destined for the most noble riders. This center was in Lipizza, a small village near Trieste. For this, he obtained stallions from Andalusia, in Spain, as well as Danish and Neopolitan mares. This produced a beautiful breed of sturdy and docile white horses, coveted by all of Europe but jealously retained by the Austrians.

1685 England

In London, the naturalist Parsons has dissected a rhinoceros, whose origin is unknown. This is a very rare animal, which has not been seen in France since the reign of King Francois I.

1688 France

The Academy of science is in mourning. Claude Perrault, physician, architect, and learned naturalist, has just died in Paris at the age of 75. He died following an illness he contracted while dissecting a camel suffering from scabies. He was the brother of Monsieur Charles Perrault, member of the French Academy since 1671, who is said to be preparing *Mother Goose Tales,* a book for young children.

1692 Russia

The explorer Ibrand Ides returned from one of his travels with a very surprising story: "A scholar traveling with me to China, who claimed he went every year to find mammoth teeth, told me that he found in the frozen ground the intact head of one of these extinct animals, whose flesh was barely rotted. Tusks protruded from its skull like those of an elephant. He and his companions had great difficulty in pulling them out, along with some bones of the head and neck that were still stained with blood. As he continued to search the ground, he discovered a monstrously big frozen foot, which he brought back to Touroukhansk."

1695 Austria

After having tried to revive the sport of hunting rabbits with cheetahs as is done in the Orient, the Emperor Leopold I decided to abandon this type of hunting, judged too bloody by the ladies and princes of his entourage.

News from New France...

1610

This year alone, French trappers have exported 15,000 beaver skins to France from trading posts along the St. Lawrence River.

1620

This year the Caen Company has sent us 20,000 beaver skins.

1670

Jean Talon, the administrator of New France for the past five years and the first to hold that position, noted in a report to Monsieur Colbert that the Iroquois, enemies of the French, have sold £120,000 worth of beaver skins to New England. An English royal charter has just officially recognized The Adventurers of England trading into Hudson's Bay, also called the Hudson's Bay Company. This is a strong competitor of our French companies.

1672

Louis de Buade, Count of Frontenac, has succeeded Jean Talon as administrator. In a report, he deplored the dealings of the French fur traders. He also wrote to Monsieur Colbert: "To tell you quite frankly, the Jesuits themselves are as concerned with the conversion of beaver as they are with that of souls."

...and from New England

Trappers from the French company called One Hundred Partners have learned from the Cree Indian hunters how the employees of the Hudson's Bay Company acquire from them the greatest number of beaver skins at the best price. When an Indian wants a gun, he has to trade pelts. Since the best guns are the long rifles, the transaction is performed according to the length of the gun. The rifle is held vertically, butt to the floor, and the Indian wishing to acquire it must pile up his pelts until the heap reaches the gun's tip. When he thinks he has attained the level, the agent of the company orders an employee to climb on top of the pile and pack it down even more. And it is always the fattest and heaviest Englishman of the post who performs this task.

Due to difficulties in trading for other animal pelts, a currency smaller than the usual beaver skin has been created in several posts of the trading company. Each of these coins represents a fraction of the value of a high-quality beaver skin. The traders of the company call these coins "beavers." They give the Indians a certain number of coins according to the value of the skins they bring in: 12 for a big and beautiful beaver skin, 12 for a bear skin, 10 for a lynx, 25 for a sea otter, 10 for a red fox, 50 for a silver fox, 10 for a marten, 5 for a mink, one half for an ermine, and one quarter for a muskrat. In exchange for the coins, the Indians can purchase whatever they wish at a well-defined exchange rate: one yard of wool flannel is worth 4 coins; a blanket is worth 10; a thick wool shawl, 20; and so on. With this system, beavers will probably have disappeared before the finances of the English kingdom are restored.

The nature and uses of the beaver

Commenting on this print from his work published in 1669 and entitled *Report on the Natural History of Animals*, Claude Perrault teaches us the true nature of the beaver: "The tail is what caused the beaver to be placed among the amphibious animals. It has no relation to the rest of the body and appears to be more closely related to the character of fish than to that of terrestrial animals. When the beaver is skinned, the scales fall off but their shape remains imprinted on the skin. The part of the skin that had the scales is very white and like that of a fish such as a porpoise or a fox-shark. While dissecting the tail, we discovered that its flesh was rather fat and very similar to that of big fish."

Those who are interested in this animal, which is said to be very abundant in New France, may read the book published in 1671 by Sir Bernardin Buchinger, Abbot of Lucelle in Alsace, entitled *Book of Ecclesiastical Cooking*. He tells of a supposedly excellent recipe for preparing the tails and paws of beavers with a black sauce.

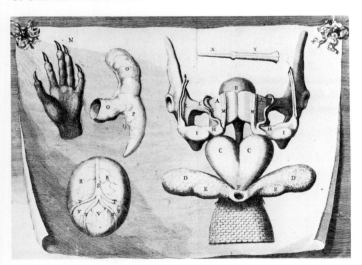

Photo P-H Plantain

In 1698 M. H. van Loon, an engraver, printed a beautiful map of North America drawn up by Nicholas de Fer and dedicated to the Dauphin. It shows the entire territory presently occupied by the French of New France. In one of the corners, a colony of beavers are depicted at work, with the following explanation:

"Their skill in building dams to retain water and to turn a small stream into a big lake in order to build their homes around it is remarkable: (A) Woodcutters who with their teeth fell large trees across the stream to serve as the foundation for their dams. (B) Carpenters cutting branches. (C) Carriers of wood for the construction. (D) Those who make mortar. (E) Commander or architect. (F) Inspector of the disabled. (G) Those who drag the mortar on their tails. (H) Beavers whose tails hurt from having worked too hard. (I) Masons who build the dams. (L) How they tap with their tails to make the masonry more solid. (M) Beavers' dome-shaped lodge with one exit on land and one in the water."

Photo P-H Plantain

The writer Monsieur de La Fontaine has described the beaver well in the ninth book of his *Fables*, published in 1679. His discourse to Madame de la Sabliere on the beaver's intelligence follows:

> . . . In that land they build their dams and dikes
> To slow the ravaging torrent of the river
> And link the bank on one side to the other.
> Their work withstands the test of time and water;
> After a bed of wood comes a bed of mortar.
> Each beaver works, for common is the task—
> The old urge on the young without rest;
> The many chiefs direct, with cudgels kept nearby . . .
> They raise their homes above the winter's ice;
> They cross the ponds on well-constructed dikes,
> The results of their labors, clever works of art.
> The men there gaze upon these works in vain;
> The beavers' knowledge is not known to them—
> When they would cross the river, they must swim.
> I could not be convinced by all mankind
> That these beavers are just body and no mind. . . .

Glossary

Absolutism A type of government in which the ruler's power is not restricted in any way

Agriculture Farming

Architecture The science or art of building

Aristocracy Any class that is considered superior because of birth, culture, or wealth

Arsenal A place where military weapons and ammunition are stored, manufactured, or repaired

Artillery The mounted guns and cannon used by an army

Astronomy The science of the sun, moon, planets, and stars

Bayonet A blade that can be attached to the muzzle of a gun

Canal A waterway that has been dug through land to provide a means of transportation

Cavalry Soldiers who fight on horseback

Cistern A tank used to store water

Civil war A war in which two groups of citizens from the same country fight with each other

Cob house A house built of material composed of clay, gravel, and straw

Colony A settlement made in another land by people who have left their own country, but who are still citizens of their own country

Dueling An organized fight between two opponents using swords or firearms as their weapons

Edict A decree

Epidemic The rapid spreading of a disease so that a large number of people have it at one time

Famine A lack of food in an area; a time of starvation

Flagellant A person who whips himself for religious discipline or for penance

Galleon A large sailing ship used by the Spanish for carrying treasure and cargo from the Americas

Government The rule or authority over a country or state

Grenadier A soldier who threw grenades

Huguenot A French-speaking Protestant of the 1500s or 1600s

Hygiene Practices that promote cleanliness and good health

Import To bring into a country for sale or use

Infantry Soldiers who have been trained, equipped, and organized to fight on foot

Leprosy A chronic bacterial disease that causes ulcers and white scaly scabs to appear on the skin; also affects the nervous system and causes muscles to become weak and deteriorate

Mercenary A soldier who has been hired to fight in a foreign army

Metallurgy The science or art of working with metals

Microscope A device that uses a lens to make small things appear larger

Mining The digging of coal or ores from a mine

Mint A place where money is made by public authority

Musket A gun used in the 16th century before the rifle was developed

Musketeer A soldier who was armed with a musket

New World Refers to North and South America

Nobility Those who are of high birth, title, or rank

Peasant A farmer in the working class

Persecute To treat a person or persons badly

Pilfer To steal things in small quantities

Pirate A person who attacks ships and then robs them

Plague A dangerous disease that quickly spreads and frequently causes many deaths

Privateer A privately owned ship that is authorized by the government to attack and capture enemy ships

Protestant A person who belongs to one of several Christian churches that have broken away from the Roman Catholic Church since the 16th century

Puritans Members of the Church of England who wanted stricter morals and simplified forms of worship during the 16th and 17th centuries

Slavery The state of one person being owned by another

Stock exchange A place where stocks and bonds are bought and sold

Tapestry A fabric into which has been woven an ornamental design or a picture

Telescope A device that makes far-off objects appear closer and larger

Textile A woven or knit fabric

Trade The buying and selling of goods or other commodities

Witch A woman who is thought to be under the influence of spirits and to have magical powers

Index

1 2 3 4 5 6 7 8 U 88 87 86 85 84 83